Nextness

wordslabs

Nextness

wordslabs – Randee Silv

New York

Nextness
Copyright © 2023 Randee Silv. All Rights Reserved.

A special thanks to Otoliths, Posit, Bone Bouquet, Datura, Word For/Word, dancing girl, illiterature, Cabinet of Heed, Maudlin House, & Urban Grafitti, where some of these wordslabs first appeared.

ARTEIDOLIA PRESS
New York

arteidolia.com/arteidolia-press

First Edition
Library of Congress Control Number: 2023902359
ISBN: 978-1-7369983-8-0

You never know what's inside a zippered secret compartment.

WORD SLABS

Disarray ... 1
Commotion ... 2
Dispatch ... 3
Untitle ... 4
Unforseen ... 5
Avenues ... 6
Sidenotes ... 7
Compact ... 8
Barrages ... 9

Example ... 10
Scarcity ... 11
Enormities ... 12
Enclosures ... 13
Relishing ... 14
Flunctuating ... 15
Contour ... 16
Buzzing ... 17
Effortless ... 18

Excursions ... 19
Blockades ... 20
Scissorkicks ... 21
Notable ... 22
Props ... 23
Expansive ... 24
Stints ... 25
Traps ... 26
Arcs ... 27

Burlap ... 28
Scrapings ... 29
Unsuspected ... 30
Nextness ... 31
Territories ... 32
Shivering ... 33
Wading ... 34
Dividing ... 35
Capsulized ... 36
Avalanches ... 37

Roughhews ... 38
Forecasts ... 39
Rattlings ... 40
Evoking ... 41
Clamps ... 42
Surpass ... 43
Between ... 44
Lessenings ... 45

Overstepping ... 46
Falling ... 47
Conduit ... 48
Bouyant ... 49
Overall ... 50
Retraced ... 51
Treading ... 52
Reveal ... 53
Intervals ... 54
Ceiving ... 55

ON>or=OFF ... 56
Unsavory ... 57
Efficiency ... 58
Access ... 59
Adjacencies ... 60
Mesmerized ... 61
Mishmosh ... 62
Faucetless ... 63
Rehashing ... 64

Trumpeting ... 65
Blending ... 66
Detach ... 67
Drenched ... 68
Wedged ... 69
Turbulence ... 70
Align ... 71
Quenched ... 72
Forfeits ... 73

Tampering ... 74
Forestall ... 75
Slapdash ... 76
Capacity ... 77
Doggedness ... 78
Zero ... 79
Altering ... 80
Creases ... 81
Crosscuts ... 82

Disarray: She's still dissecting stems, insects, blossoms and vines for furthermores and likewise seamlessly framed. Short dashes long dashes fault perpetual alterations intentionally exposed. Suddenly savored surges artfully flop. Rethinking maneuvers goes on indefinitely. Recalling what remained had to be memorized. Hampered whisperings way too extreme. She picked up a seashell and heard screechings & squawks. Obsolete jottings caught but not captured. Advancing priorities with no introductions no final scenes. Weathered interference is wickedly haunting. It can't be fixed. But un tie ing would do.

Commotion: A face. The same face that repeated itself on what he was wearing resembled the man sitting across from me. The similarities were hard to ignore. One smiled and one didn't. He held a ticket and what he carried was carefully knotted shut. The ticket was almost identical to the one I was holding. I knew we hadn't been at/to/in the same place but we could've been. Variousness crumbled into racket. Rumbles competed with clanging. Listening intersects and pulled out. There's never a shortage of temptation to intervene with what's overheard. She was begging her not to give in even if it appeared obvious. Again. And again. And again. A floundering loss. Agonizing & weary. Nobody likes not knowing. People should and do talk in code. Birds backtracked as we crossed the river. The announcement wasn't very clear. Maybe objects can swim faster than you think.

Dispatch: Unsettled sways are not themselves. Steering thru beveled hubs, thru electrified spawnings, we never were. But we are. Encoded with imports and exports and so forths. Specifics depict zilch nada nil. Webbed in untold claims, you, I, roused by obscure bounties. Venture ravishing revamps. Possibly. Verifying dismissed declines. Possible. Centermost setbacks elevate watchtower mischances. Sliding forays nullify triggers. He skips that part as to who clement pastures thrive. No reenactments. No miscalculations. A luminous gale.

Untitle: You could be persuaded by inescapble fragilities, by glorified kinks that fizz. You should be urged by estimations stored in seethrough cylinders or by dwindling passages that sag from pins & tacks. I total carouselled kalediscopes as they gracefully float. Irreversible ticking. A slamming. Flurries of absences blanket an arid bleakness that does expire, that does wane. Populated shakenings are sighted. Curvable outtakes dig the deepest by choice. Invalidating. Overruling. Overturning reined in. Bonded to rooftops definitions redefined.

Unforeseen: We're told pleasure fulfills itself. Nothing is non-available. No need to rehire. Weeds tumble essentially to get somewhere. Where they end up has little to do with kisses from a zillion spring buds washed away in muddied inlets minus ions & eons. Corralled riddles puncture & probe beyond alabaster roofs. Chatter is noticeably taut. Too much is nested. Too much gets clipped. Barred meanderings automatically swallowed. The nays keep wrestling in a three cornered ring. Shes and hes rescue caged doves from patinaed gourds. No one can remember when the crescendoing started. Crowds will not voluntarily retreat.

Avenues: Three times. Six times. Twenty times over. Seasonable cadences peer and pry from sunup to dawn. Groundless. Needless. Needless useless. There's this monotonous pulling apart of overrated portals hardened hard. Lustering gapes. Painted soot. Circadian stormings rummage through craving whims mid to halfway. The event, the same event wipes trivial bellows from memory. Yours. Mine. Erratic. Akin. It just can't be this and then that and that then. Coincidences noted. Recorded henceforth. Lone motifs muse over ditching. Heed. Yield. Disable. Unotherings. Unotherings. It's not a misspelling.

Sidenotes: The ceiling rendered her speechless. To compare backing up with backing off is simply off topic. Comments overdramatic. Comically cramped. Skittish pursuits stapled to polished debates. No reason to sun on velvet lawns. Tangible arenas. Unlatched gates. Substitutes can't be swallowed. She's shuffling facts and accuracy like a deck of cards. Requiries succumb to scramblings. Beaded circumstances trade one for the other. You can't convert checkerboard seams into somber locomotions or rocky ledges. Uniform and unchanging they do not become. Quietness is not silent. There's a large uproar. She's holding a whisk without a bowl. Xxaggerations simultaneously dodge. Explaining things will be the subject of her next talk.

Compact: It wasn't really an impasse, deadlock or stalemate, but what was did not halt. Breaks, cracks, gaps. Seven tabulations. It can't be explained. The sky, though. That was dauntingly clear. I looked over her shoulder at what she'd written. "The lobby was dotted with frying pans and potted ferns and there were things on the table and things on the wall." Horns. Not the ones to heed alarms. Tools without purpose. Some plastered, unplastered. All clutteredly arranged. The light switch didn't budge. They packed up and so did she. Farness dripped steadily into remoteness. If you want, you can exchange places and look at what they see. Time brought storms. Storms brought quivers. They did make it across. Everything strokes a memory. Everything recalls a sensation. She motions fiercely. He and he next to me, we tried not to blink. Coldness never seems to thaw. They might as well have had speared the ice. How do you not fold into hate? Shovel it. Shovel it. Shovel it. I refused to pound the table. Distracted by distraction. The scent of mint tea was everywhere.

Barrages: Siding with fleets of undertakings, variegated and divergent, I don't have it backwards. Warned against murkiness. Inflatable contrarieties. Tepid dismantlings cloak in telescopic scrawls. Mistimed sequels bidding for someone else. I gravitate toward formations of carved eclipses. I tug. I heave. Neon washed havings blind scripted thresholds decades too late. Crystalline resilience propels. It's fervent. It's swift. With the heat of the wind I replay the speed of the river. Lastingness remains consistent. I don't have it backwards.

Example: He said he was not an optimist but a prisoner of hope. He said he was an instrument at the juncture before nothing made any sense. He did get me thinking about how things that are on can then be off. I stood beside her not knowing why anything is anything, not knowing what cements with and without. Something had caused the palm trees to wither. She rallied us in. We climbed over a rope, a barrier, a checkpoint. He held his footing on a makeshift throne slicing away contradictions buried in muck. She played for him. She danced for him. The deepest point of the root is where the sap is. He hadn't done it before so he's doing it now. Savage or wild, no one was sure. Quirky or plotted. Nobody cared. He had it all figured out except where did nothing come from. Oranges. A bushel of oranges rolled towards, faster, then stopped.

Scarcity: Dicey clusters bear no resemblance. Lookouts perch upon detectible interference. Closed forms. Arches swell from min to max. Seated. Bunched. Spotted. Feverish cores knock over self contained strongholds hung from spigots & draining pegs whisked across wind tunnels. Reflections burn what can not grow.

Enormities: According to her shes and hes, reciprocal porosities convey supple instances. Farseeing. Vigorously sporadic. Closely related to unanimous treasures that cling to chasms to flumes. Toward jarring terrene furrowed mergers on iron curbent locales. Favored spanning insertions. Her mode, her trend shields carbon copies of discordant pairings. Comprised. Upheld. I chart misaligned redundancies. I reinstate non linear brickbat. I track upshoots and upshots that falsely rate stowaway renditions. Vanity flights. Insofar. Insofar as unresolved existence bound schemes need to transcend.

Enclosures: I sat down on a chair without an "X". Rewrites stricken from pebbled idling laid on thick. They're not paying attention. Nuances tip consumption toward luring red hot embers. Perfumed stoppages should've crumbled into gullies & moats by now. But. But. But. Piercing grips mold jeweled editions glued to PR hypes. Episodes of consequences from tableau to solitude. Vicinities only rumored. Transparent. Entireties disappear. Road maps exceed microscopic certainties. Synchronize. Pool. Amplify. Condors will return to the Northwest.

Relishing: Braided into feathered vistas, upwellings divide surfaces with shatterable forbiddenness. Spotables on file tag reversing cascades as porous catchalls. Byproducts taped. Catalogued. Chronicled. They're. They are. There. There. When. Then. Central cores skirt perimeters with cumbersome sidesweeps. Downhill coasting ossifies montaged abundant dints. Defined by. Followed by. Surrounded by. Protrusions and manufactured disturbances pawn duped spinoffs of leafy spurge. Assemblages persistent. Ebbing planetary squared meters roost on an offset calm. A thousand whyfors why.

Fluctuating: Pickles & pies a la carte at the Take Ten Lounge. Splendid. Massive. Bold. He wasn't kidding. Celestial winks strictly overdue. Her shes collaged candied tempos pencilled in. I rearrange wasting waste combining combinations ticklishly abridged. Coolness marinates on skeleton whorls. Whimsical signals ride scolding brims that rhyme with skirting beaked thirsts. Decal interims of chancy monologues. Clumsy removals are getting worse. The observer. The observed. Her ovations. Her bows. Yonders fuel hithers. Hit refresh.

Contour: Permanence entangles. Existence entwines. Sedimentation hypnotic. Portraits are not descriptions. Things do fall to be picked up. Consumption might be inconvenient. She said no one has the luxury of retreat. I don't want to mislabel or relabel agendas of theft not yet thinkable. Artificial night curdles at steadfast speeds. I can't omit. I can't ignore. Heroes. He doesn't want to be one. Fresh black. Dull black. Sensual black. Equalizing present past should make you flinch. Twelve stood handcuffed. Two headed north. You can strangle fairness and duplicate neglect. You can count days intoxicated from sunken logs and mechanical howls. You can wander through the forest bumping into trees. You can stage whatever surfaces. Troupe. Alliance. Coalition. Majestic silence.

Buzzing: Full scale. Full blown. Slandering sneers imitate vogue. Uninvited nods marinate barnacled contraptions. All the shes converge on dittoed sums of fusty say-so-s till they rupture. Mangoes don't lead to barbecues nor do bullseye stomps. He's gotta be seething. Artificialized quests of staccato scorecards post tuned out shrugs in keepsake cellars. Necktie guilded clubs brushed aside rock bottom. Peppery spectrums reek from shingled grooves. Hitchhiking sacred chards got him nabbed. Her magnified bronze torso was eagerly pelted & egged. Cause. Effect. Chains of events.

Effortless: Not enough flows backwards after having been received. The longer I neared, more toppled. Boxed in, below, out & above, a forced curve floods garnished sediment. He's shaking. She is, he is. He's collecting scraps, accumulating, accelerating. He discloses. She, she, he. He guarantees that nothing has been touched. She was there and then there was she. One follows the other. She thought about him sitting in a doorless meadow. His name not asked. Steps slow, mouth covered. A taste. I don't imagine sweet. Puzzled. Not knowing where. Where to. Where when. A slight initial twist. One circle to another circle. Trappings narrow as hoarded bribes are assumed unthreaded. Rotations short. A cord's length oils a stockpile of gathered harvests. I'm sitting in his seat next to his. They are both not here. Slashed left shredded left scorched left spun.

Excursions: Things like that. Just like that. Typical microcosmic jammings. Pretending. Impersonating. A manicured invisibility. A surly lavishness. Mollified quashes posturing. Posing. It's a spectacle for matinee idols. It's a pageant for gibbering rigamarole. It's an avalanche fluent in dualized airplay keyed and intractable. Swells nudge. Prod. Poke. Serrated elements escalate gestures at the onset of overgrown quandaries. He intercedes. She intervenes. Asphalt mounds roost on teeming havoc. Billowing eddies sponged bare.

Blockades: She jotted down notes. He tapped his forehead. Neither knew why. There has to be more to it than chiseled squares and open palates. Okay, so I was eavesdropping. Those two were going at it arguing about $$ collected. Tugging, pushing. They stopped before it got bloody. The plan, to dematerialize, but they didn't know if they could. Broken specks and slivers might never re-glue. Seconds advanced. Minutes withdrew. It's hard to believe there's an ending before it ever began. Now I know why he tried to enter from the rear. He started upper left and ended bottom right. Her feet were solid on the ground. He answered questions on the ins and outs of collapsable seeded theories. The pluses and pitfalls. His sounded redundant and not all that informative on how to reach the outer banks. I threw his suitcase six stories down. All I could make out were ashtrays superimposed on passing faces. Rubbing thins. He sang to himself and then to us. He said that it took nine hours of her doing it. If that milk bottle isn't really a bottle of milk, he tells me, I'm still going to use it. They wanted to boycott. But not today.

Scissorkicks: Nay. Negotiable. Nope. Lightning strikes the smell of neglect. Echoes wander. (Day)dreaming. (Day)tripping. Compass points unleashed for eternity start off the week in 2nd position. A single book hangs from a clothesline waiting. Soaked. Scripted. I hurry into a run. Seared contentions spill into memoed crevices. Scenarios switched after emptied rotate collectibles hurling at paper lanterns. Backgrounds posing for foregrounds crawl as slow as caterpillars chasing slugs. Doubts stare into mine. Potholes. Tracking holes. Buttonholes. Etcetera etcetera. Forget-me-knots act as cover.

Notable: Blank. Then much occurred. Predictable meaninglessness runs amok. Capsized reversals take refuge in riddled starkness. Translucent sturdy emits foraged noir timbre. Could be feasible. Even plausible. Slit. Sliced. Unshakeable noontides wafer thin. Somehow or other there's a crystalizing, a bond. The day. Extraordinary. I'm thinking about what I shouldn't be thinking about. Nowheres and elsewheres. I lean away only to be caught in an immediate afterwards. Footsteps. Freefalls. Nosedives.

Props: I don't think they were assembled to be reversible. The seams had already begun to fray. I don't know why she watered down what was supposed to have taken place. Overly leery & overly guarded. It was as if she'd been told to. Sweetness. It can swarm around you. Could be that I'm ducking him right now. Resisting a like to an unlike. Resisting the debris, the residue. It was like riding a seesaw. Gates rolled down since closing. A handprint, maybe an off centered heart. A footprint, maybe a thickened zero were freshly positioned on brick exteriors. He came closer, squatted down and tapped somebody's shoe. He didn't bother to compliment her outfit. Wearing a dime store crown but holding no torch he greeted passing cars. Piled up cartons had tumbled over. He just kept adding wet coats of leftover paint, layer after layer, each a varying degree of the same hue. I could hear him laughing in the bathtub. He said everything was fine except that his lips tingled. I tried picturing a stage. Two ping pong balls going back and forth with an old recording of him and I and I and him. You never know what's inside a zippered secret compartment.

Expansive: She rose when she reached the brink. They said that it shouldn't be washed if it's prized, that you should overtake the how despite the when. Performances replace stunts. Stunts mimic performances. They map the distilling of vinegar. Flocks of hyenas. Herds of harpoons. More filled in. Allure. Counterfeit. Forbidden. Rapid marks needlessly trample dawn's crisscrossing. He unrolled his masterpiece with the most original speech. If one fires, they will all fire. Maybe one will withdraw.

Stints: Another sunken mudbath. Another immobile corridor. Punctuated declarations rank exit signs. Farther. Further. The bearer shuns the receiver. The receiver rallies the bearer. Trophies. Gems. Unsold thrills. Broadly absent but readily concurring. Kind of. Not exactly. Dim interiors tighten. Cellophane mazes clock ornamental blunders. Echoic quells. Vertical decent. Wheelbarrows. Alleys. Trampolines race up tiresome slopes. Wherefore. Therefore. Thereupons. I lay a fallen starfish on a desolate fringe. Squint and you'll probably miss it.

Traps: Mud. Rubbish. Dirt. Souvenirs can always be bought. Inventions can always be invented. Appearances penetrate high up on the hill. A square, a rectangle, pose the same vertical cut short. Twisted wire blackboard ramblings bake into ticking pendulums swallowed by chatterings left to graze at a distance. Eruptions overflow as promised. Ousting gravity soothes sluggish intent. Flashbacks unreliable. She asked if silence was accurate. Courtyards. Woodsheds. I went in.

Arcs: Four undercovers got in smelling like wire twirled rust. Frigid plunders. Humorless formalities. Checkered boulevards disguise disfigured dissent. Syncopated. Unwanted. Trite & tiring spectacles jump from behind. Loud streams of narrowing instantly swell. Tossing out or tossing in necessities concealed by yesterday's applause sets off voltage edgy and blunt. Second guessing aftereffects creep crawl towards nothing decided. Persons. Beings. Pale celadon misplaced curvatures. She kept asking if I had it. I don't have it and I didn't see it. Fairness. I keep meditating on fairness.

Burlap: Lizards feast on burnt crust casted from bartered coins and sea dung. Mangrove roots rotate in descending sequences. Prolonged chants ferment in rusty bowls weighing somewhat less than the moon. No wind. Swamp. No boat. Canyon. Shredded crimes and battered longings nailed shut. Nostalgic foes harpoon ashes anchored in muggy damp air. His seemed urgent. She's quieter than he. I slide to the end. Blame. Rage. Do species exist to be extinct? Haunted. Half drowned. Nobody ever told him. Nobody knew. I too kissed the hairy larva of a butterfly.

Scrapings: Flimsy levers. Flimsy bolts. Gone & unturned. I hear the current rise higher and higher. Thundering embankments splinter. There are worthless bravos fisted chants and patterned auras. Minutes push. Hours haul. She felt the breath of apparitions sooner than expected. It might occur. It might dissolve. Stomping feet isn't enough. Night is not a pantomime. Someone tell them that. In next soon eventually tires. There was a tunnel overhead instead of below. Miniature cosmologies wash ashore. Frustrations mount. I repeated what she repeated what they repeated. Vapor freezes. Life frozen. Sideshows sold out. Fresh mementos are already in place.

Unsuspected: Plot: continual. Rising action. Downward action. Climax mundane. It was hard to know what he was weighing. Instinct. Passion. Delirium. Twirling pushed him forward. They gawked at him — the shadows that lived on the street — as he mimicked them in flight. "Stifling and revolting" they must've heard him say. I sat by the pond and counted ducks, quivers, brisk steps. He'd been told that his father was her father although it might've been a lie. The day was acting somewhat normal until the phone rang. Frantic. Racing. Guesses jagged. Each more certain. Each more potent. They knew it to be true. There'd be a record, an investigation. Arousing false flaws might dangerously incite madness. He'd seen this all before. He held back from asking it but then he did. No closer to knowing. There would be a lot of waiting. A heart is not like a box. It folds and unfolds. He said that the clouds hadn't settled yet and the sky, the sky didn't know what shade of blue to be.

Nextness: Knowingly destined to change only slight, she / like them, stark, firm / takes just seconds in the elevator. Earsplitting thunder scrambles parched systems stashed into discolored heaps pushing & pulling more than can be blotted. Rehearsals of squatting. Of hauling. Amplified. Cursed. Vice versa. She didn't know why. Rolling and rolling. Hardly a lapse. Hardly a breath. Locked stares rival replacements. Silhouettes coated with red marrow revert to a rising current. Encores. There always are. Too many forevers you can't pierce. Violent, violet, it doesn't seem to matter.

Territories: Planned measured delivered. Bending shifting shocking. Attending blanking scrubbed. You could feel the crispness of consuming and the distraction of error. He talked about replication. She talked about unsealing. He stepped. He stepped. He paused. He hadn't gotten very far. She recited a section about constant leaving. She rejected modular vulgarity. Slippages details modification. Filtering reducing calculating. People eat and drink at different speeds. Square table with a manuscript. They rested bewilderedly detached. Divvying erasing proclaiming. Everyone carries something different. Everyone everyone everyone. There I said it. Delays. They do more than hold us up. She combs his hair ever so gently. Recounting memories. We all do it. Locating whereabouts. We all do that too. I thought about asking her where she was. His liquored breath complimented mine. Two helicopters against a white paper napkin. I heard her crying as I left. A tangled mess. Slightly changed. He chops. I disregard.

Shivering: In one gate and out through another. Back in and out more than twice. Motives obviously unreliable. Lightning. Celebration. Tilting the odds he said. Is it true that the average person lies three times within the first 10 minutes of meeting a stranger? I turned. I don't know why. Holding firm on the ground fluently in sync with a newly planted linden she thought she heard a trumpet player soloing around the corner. Trampling gusts bombarded chatter from the evening's downpour. Women of erotic grace gazed upwards. Each leaned on one foot and cradled a simple sphere. They were accused of outward ridicule for wearing primitive faces and dancing about. No matter what they would not halt. It was pretty dark in the room. Only a faint light streaming in from the neighbor's kitchen. I must have heard the knock at the door because I was standing there. I had to have swung it open. The hallway looked exactly like it should. The chill in the air was finally all I could think about. Someone asked if I could run faster than a dragonfly.

Wading: Significant timing. Always about to be. Extra layers barge in saturating could've beens. Tinseled strings. Putty. Chance. Shaded exposures dart bottlecaps darting oystercatchers. Freshly lit variants roam unrehearsed. Spatially absorbent. Susceptible. Cosmic. Atmospheric hilarities earmark her iffy sprees her lace drawn mappings her pending afterwords. Horizoned snags kin to pillared jetties salvage exclamation marks from foreshadowing windowsills. Partnered invitations. Clashing fluidity bridged. Volleys of hazy out of focus laments warp into a fiery easiness.

Dividing: They were bothered that I'd nestled in so close behind them. The tips of my fingers accidentally brushed against the back of his neck and they didn't like that. She kept sipping hot soup with dipped bread. I wanted to hear. Hear how she breaks lines into quartered halves. Seven minutes and we were still not moving. I didn't peg him as a long distance runner, a push-poller or a discus thrower. Whatever they were reaching for must have been kicked under the seat. Heading towards hollowness. He told them he had lived in a cave, though not which one. Doubts. They all had doubts. He trapped himself differently than a rabbit or a fox. I thought she and her were the same. Both wore puffy skirts and boasted of appetites seductively unscheduled. He hesitated but didn't delay. She saw it so he saw it. She waved to come in as if she knew me. Her mind must have changed. A yes flipped to a no. Her finger swayed back and forth without the clicking of a metronome. I'd never seen eyes opened so wide as he took aim. He stood with his bald head and fired four shots into water that hadn't been weeded or drained. Her strokes were fast and steady. Stones that don't hold sticks tumbled from her pockets. She rubbed them fiercely. It was hard not to notice the smell. She was there with them. It could have been like that.

Capsulized: Blood on napkin. Paradise on shirt. A magician's dove flies from a traveling pushcart. Targeted. Jammed. Unborn rags birth from her belly. Strange vanishings traded on dismembered grids. I let each out of its paper bag. Re-inhabit. Re-lodge. Checkered sequins trash bottomless pillars. Flowering vines fail to entertain. Bend as it bends. Dip as it dips. Sweet acorns clustering inside hornet nests coax out blanketed conundrums. Vastness leaves my body. Stampedes lock arms. Widespread blindness is already upon us.

Avalanches: Snide gilded frames reattach. Sleek underbrush misjudges starbursts as an exception or as a hoax. However eerie. However skintight. Unlikely legends coin transparencies sundered and razed. Myriads. Slews of tender oak scars peel anecdotes from viewers. From watchers. Opaque. Glittery. Make up your mind. Nonattempts never bloom. Robust. Dire. Clamorous. Packs of saddled girths affix to jerky brawls. Onyx padded slumbers leak hasbeen theorems. She scraps entrenched absurdity. Reeking offerings. Sommeraults fastened to hemispheric departures. A quieterness morphs into porcupine quills.

Roughhews: Pungent disinterest never promised much to begin with anyway. Umpteen wherewithals churn into glossy voiceovers hidden behind moth eaten antics. Doubled grasps seduce circularity on russet sidewalks. Prolonged influx. Clogged. Hedged. Simmering flares submerged in camouflaged secrecy. Replantings & quickenings & preambled tidal pools reroute despite vine clad murmurs. Hardcore headstrong cringes search madly for jettied burrows idle slack. Blistery aromas. Lush vacated eternities weigh unmoved. Straddling throngs of dents. Of nicks. Barely seen foliage takes a morning plunge.

Forecasts: I wasn't really spinning, more pushing up as I turned down. I was supposed to be in the sea not in an hourglass under feathered timber. Stunted. Oblong. She went on defining purple grays that cluster at the verge of dawn. She said it was absolutely the same, damn it, the same instrument, the same gadget. They could be named no matter how outrageous or outraged. Tenderness slides sometimes beneath the chair. She writes that down. Divisions and subtractions suffocate adding. Cruelty has no favorites. Ashes are ashes. Inevitable disguises veer from a course with meanings never kept. She dreams like you. Never asked. She never answered. Repeated repetitions repeating.

Rattlings: There is a visible crack. There are accompanying characters. Threaded paper twists into minuscule eyelets. Hammering snarls divvy swapped ashes stung by thises. By thats. Objeks. Frazzled laments lay explicitly deserted. Sloping slants flatten upright. She said she was a bird not a butterfly pressed between two pages. Onlooking residue. Stupefying bleakness missed in the rush. Somewheres verging on nowheres wither under rolling tumbleweeds.

Evoking: Sand-storms. Electric-storms. Crowd-storms. Bellyflops stamped return to sender broadcast in the metro. I climb into a smaller circle and then an even smaller one. Shooting stars stop mattering. Salamanders still haven't budged from basement lakes. Iridescent sirens porous & pressed tally nested grins. Fossilized sequences heisted from moderate to light to heavy. Traded flip flops dumped into gambling ringsides Clabbering rituals absurdly excessive. Hoops appear. 700 so far reported.

Clamps: She stared at a wooden plank and trembled when it trembled. She moved over only with reluctance. The whys, the whats never given. Ascending latitudes absorbably gnarly. Monotone narrations loom. A piling of piles. The squirming of squirms. Encased in spellbound stupor there's this replaying of dormant rhymes. Archless nooks with miscued circuitries leave no leeway. Outshouting. Overshouting. I, like others, devour exhales strikingly laughable from inflatable dustbins. Dicey. Crafty. Sinkable. Not at all substantial.

Surpass: I watched him squeeze & squeeze, empty & refill gushes of toned down acidic scarcity. Sleeping serpents quadrupled in size wrap around ghostly indentations. Insatiable outbursts. I brush static under static. Copykats wrestle meteorites on doubly dizzifying magnetic rails. Miles retake miles. It can be seen. Said. Can be done. I don't want to strike what she desires what she inhabits what she divulges. Constructing identical sameness makes them flinch. I don't agree that it can be stretched like a rubber band. I heard a deep unruffled voice but couldn't see where. The time was an hour ahead and he an hour behind. Clearance dances about. She never left. She was never there. Primal alertness is right in front. Milk turns to glue. Everything burns too fast. Nothing hides unless you see it that way.

Between: A thick woolen scarf tightly wrapped around her even with plenty of warm heat. I don't know what made me decide to watch that locked gaze of hers as she swayed more to some than to others. The serenade of three buskers norteños took me back under sculpted laurel trees where towering stacks of sombreros balanced on heads while they waited for sales and I waited for him. I circled 4 blocks up and 4 blocks down. The hill seemed steeper than usual but I knew it wasn't. Absent cobblestones slowed my speed. There's something about pulling away from structures & existences, about pulling away from what you've already done. Leaving and crossing eases what one can't. I leaned over the edge. Mirrored in salt breeze, lava crumpled into florescent blue. The usual interruptions on the late evening bus. There's something about overtones in a standstill. There's something about recurring slowdowns. I ignore the number of stops left. It gets tiresome wrestling with time being stretched. Pouring. Pouncing. Almost stinging. A sandy path through the cliff's sharp brush quickens. Nets & vessels yet to anchor. There's something about the dark blackness.

Lessenings: Sharpened thorns play tricks with muted echoes. Curtains pulled down on canopies still pliable. Lost among rings of rivers I stack what I can describe. I position myself so that edges touch edges. Referencing happenstance, coincidence, conjuncture, she conducts an orchestra of cicadas, seductive and charmed. She speaks of value, worth, injury, of acid and rust. Walkways taper and towering caverns fill with long fixed stares. She details the closest re-entry. Appraisals swerve farther ahead as they pass from hand to hand. Crowds hired to impress, to dazzle. Rotations gel fast. Says he's him when he knows he's not. Bitterness disbands timeworn overtures siphoned for other matters. I have to stall the clamoring of broadcasted predictions in bone orchards. She moves tiresomely from leaf to leaf. A useless use of 360 degrees.

Overstepping: Crushed into this locus of interlocking slates. Eldritch totterings. Rotational scans. Wrinkled legibility. She's chatting to him and him to her. I'm not very good at reading lips. I echoed what was unsaid. Mazy. Knotty. Jumpy. Jerky. Fluky treks. Her animated creaks. Her inhabitable barrenness ajar. Substitions half-built. Courted memoirs toy with fortunes. Quantum misfires. Funneled clichés equivalent to consumable fruitions tempt zeal and fervor and zest. Assuming assumptions. Concluding without a conclusion. Switching arbitrary inroads for low hanging scrolls. I remastered afternoon syncopations. I slid into a momentary radius breadth.

Falling: So much is falling. Nothing to grab onto unless you stand still. A single room. Undisturbed. Stormless. Maybe he was thinking about outcomes and aftermaths. Maybe he was thinking about unmarked ruins buried below. Fifteen of us watched the folding of unneeded entries parade as decrees. Tumbling. Tackling. Scattered. Promises tear apart neutrality abandoned in the marsh. Not nearly as keen. Not nearly as valid. Slides and quicks smother under assault. Articulating sabotage is a skill. Nothing is static. Meaning is the meaning. Ripening disintegrates into continuity. Inscriptions, monuments, alphabets borrowed and scratched out. Abundance deluded in sweet fields bursts through foggy glass. He crosses the state line. Canyons. Cliffs. Crevices. Frenzy is electrifying. A face is so you can make faces. Pine cones on a fig tree. Eventually you have to jump the tide.

Conduit: Monotone. Monotonous. Monopolized. Not able to decide who is which and which is what, she rests on her cane in a field of chestnuts & corn. Beautified erosions weaken. Grated upheavals undermine. If she doesn't awaken he will remind her. There is this purr when he sings. The door still hasn't loosened. He runs not very fast inside a hotel room while reciting the fine points of shipwrecks and pitchforks and manta rays. He was very talkative so I talked. Summarized abbreviations are to be unveiled every Monday. He wants her lips but the moment is spoiled. She stands in a crimson sea knee deep. A gap. A hole. Lopsided in reverse. Faint and hardly there. It was too crowded that night so I went again.

Buoyant: Log jams. Gridlock. Shortened punchlines swing from chandeliers earmarked extinct. Soft oval valleys bypass desert outcrops. I didn't mean to swipe piffled bunk. Scissored mutations stacked to farfetched lengths nibble away at luncheon counters in public squares. Mannequins plummet from crescent peaks. Brittle. Stiff. Latecomers toss boxes of triple A's & yarrow sticks. Identical laughter. Defunct relics. The resemblance was obvious. A three sided hammer hits exactly where it should.

Overall: They said he had reached a dead-end. Putting cherry pits in pockets and flies in ears seemed productive enough. Some labelled it a getup, a costume, a throwtogether. Assigned to index the sighs, the hums, the whens, the hows, she reclines next to stolen idols pulled from peat bogs awaiting messages from above. Switching catastrophes can never be completely finished. Hard right. Easy wrong. Sliding away from dimness brinking. Unsuspected prompts faithfully descend. *Ramped up in energy. Speech rapid. Desire rushing. Somewhat focused. Woke up from not sleeping. Maybe mid-day. Lightness even.* He was certain that another time would be the last time. He had forgotten why and no one could remember. She told them that the mask, the one she'd especially modeled & etched for him, no longer fit like it once had. Oppose landings on split terrains. Dissuade instant holdups. Postpone hesitation before pausing. Dark black on darker black on lighter black on whited black. If it wasn't for the walls I'd be falling into a ditch. Charms, shears, growling swirls were excluded, but I did see a ladder. In fact, I saw three. They left before they took notice.

Retraced: Catenary pendulous waves. Funhouse mirrors. Bogus remakings levitate. Reminiscing. Already complicated. She wasn't moving. Anecdotal shortages baffled even her. Plated rime. Needled columns swerve dome to dome. Unbending bends bent counterclockwise. Mudballs flung in every direction. Meltings & refreezings. Crazed volumes of sure bets. If she could remember. If she did. She'd summon what she just said. Conjectured purging is an ancient way to bargain. She wasn't waiting for a bus. She was the midnight air.

Treading: Drybeds. Reedbeds. Nobody said they were willing targets. Curbside underscores intensify forms and figures. Remarkably lame chimneyed mantels auction scribbling finalities bought rebought for yellowing dingy uphauls. Rounds and rounds of sandwiched stupor creep back into routine sight. Fed up with has been scants, his exhaustion should be your exhaustion. Her concerns yours. She lay there with them. Bundled lengthier. Taller. Showings. Proof. Anything. Anything besides the stirring of a dazed quavering vortex.

Reveal: I signed up for lessons on how to guard silence. The ad on the billboard sold me the idea. Due to popularity he said to expect that it might not be near. In fact, he said, the list had already reached capacity. "Come worship up on a hilltop on the fifth Friday of the month." "Protect & Don't Worry: Microchip your Pet." They leaned with them, their dancing partners, and cut across a darkly tinted puddle hardly touching granular exteriors. I can't tell what's moving fast. Instantly forgotten. Infinite tiers passionately ditched. Brooms sweeping while liquids boil. Nothing to bolt shut. Much too much reassessing over adulterated facts. Evidence lacking. Coincidences fluid. Perplexity doubling as brief interludes oppose permanent sealing. He is outmaneuvered and conveniently selects what to toss. Preventions fail to bypass requests that can't be shaken. He knows he has to. He pivots without a hinge.

Intervals: She didn't know how words would align as he ran in passing. She looked downward and he looked to somewhere. She traced his outlined form. Neither could describe it exactly. Further than close and farther than imagined. It was more than holding on before jumping or tightly squeezing the juice from its fruit. People get up and others sit down. Deep thoughts. No thoughts. Speaking thoughts. I do not know him. I do not know her. She doesn't know him and he's never seen her. Low haze filled the sky from smoke stacks. His tailored coat hangs beneath his knees. Hurdling a fence she takes a picture of a dog. He spikes a cherry soda. I didn't want to be sold the reasons why I should adhere. I didn't want to be sold rants that smell stale and soured. I didn't want to be sold what has already been trampled. Rows of a dozen windows. The line about building a container for toothpicks wasn't that funny.

Ceiving: Suspend. Compress. Shelve. A heaviness strangely staggering. Reminiscent undertows draped in finely tuned expansions reside within. Grill. Pump. Wring. Discounted continuum reels into speckled passageways. I waver from shadowy mists that cast a before and an after. Hollowed filaments decompose from fading teal garbs. Feverish barren proportions miscalculate stonewalled scores that should never have been. I tabulate traversing depths. I crave defiant rovings. I divert. I deflect from semi whereupons.

ON>or=OFF: Economics. No. Revolution. Yes. He. And he. Neither would alter. Fewer tickets for pubic urination have been reported. I skipped the question about incidents of theft or blackmail. Depending on sources and sizes for packaged disasters it's almost impossible to decide what to decide. Separating from recent past is no easy feat. They were convinced they could decipher his inklings and clues. He was sitting in the front row but was never asked. She kept losing her balance while trying to find her keys. He had already spelled out how she twisted the bitterness of regret. He told her if you can't see what's bucking into you, disengage. Disentangle. She told him that whichever way was not the way. Continuous continuations are like feeding the birds.

Unsavory: Rippling labyrinths. Babbling dilemmas. Lying down on flawed remainders is no excuse. More is not more. The noise out there is getting louder. Slip-ups. U-turns. After-turns. Chapter after chapter. It goes by so recklessly, so obtrusively. Contrasts negate likeness. Likenesses become sameness. Desire fulminates toward disdain. Built-in turnings. Penned-in inertia. Farewells carry lanterns with parrots instead of flames. Flaunting. Parading. Vice versa. A single dot. It seems that they didn't get the same instructions.

Efficiency: Never enough to reuse. Never enough dry blue tips or burnt ambers. Never enough words echoing on wet rocks reciting tales. Fallen groves divide what's at stake. Vacancy creeps in and out whether you ask for it or not. What can't be saved is crumpled. What can is re-straightened. He said he had slots for Saturday noon. He was not confused as they claimed. They too were decomposing. Long legs navigate no hurdles. Short legs do the same. Joining(s) and returning(s). He said what startled her had approached from the shooting range and that shipping costs will be five hundred. If you catch it, it is yours. Less motion can stifle if winter is late. Rusty metal was indeed misread. He crouches and does it again. She crouches to collect what someone else hadn't. Neither budge. I have to get up from where I'm sitting.

Access: Hurled into undrinkable levitation a calculated ridge was her swiftest closure. Unknotted smears cheapen remakes squirreled away in bulldozed stairwells. Categorizings were deliberately identified as mis-strung beaded necklaces. On deserted idyll squalls disposable assemblies infuse slated undoings. Scuttled haste obscured in copper sheathed hulls. Differing paths of dayglo hijacks. Dislodgers. Dislocaters. Disuniters. Unjustness, a dirty deal. Unfairness is unfair. Embers from latchless cinders flame ballads with unmistakable precision. The only difference. A seeded stroke stretches toward the marrows.

Adjacencies: Leafing through barbed clipts. Fermenting blockouts. Usable jultings gang up as rendezvous near. Falsified quirks typify pleated immensities. Your prouncements. Your dealings. It's your laxness barreling into heedlessness. She keeps encircling that torsoed mannequin. She insists it looks like her. Inadvertently uninventive. Obtuse summits ravel to concede. Off ramps meld blusterous levels of occupied taunts. Garnered fusions. Bewitched comings and goings amplify what's what. Acclaimed lures haphazardly cave into mimeoed dissuasions. I trim what hasn't survived. A jostle that won't do.

Mesmerized: Some talk about it more than others. Some are left to argue with the ground. She pointed to groupings. A racket of probabilities. Attempted vs. doing. In. Inside. Insideness. She condensed fading momentum into freewheeling quotations. Pretty slick. Five exchangeable variations. Mark down. Take down. Beat down. Wounded stumps retrieve hazards lyrically unruly. Tear. Torn. Composed nuances excavate randomly from tattered pulp. Uprooted categories finish before starting. Mistaken for a straightened unwinding folded flame I fell doubly quick into its vacant awe.

Mishmosh: The remodeling of consumed omissions. The rerouting of unsigned blares. Snapshots emulate teacups. Press clippings pinned to rugs. Fabricated pretense solidifies buckling sneers. Deafening. Maddening. Being consumed was never the motif. Flashbacks fizzle in the undertow few can cite. This is dot dot dot anonymously removed. This could be dot dot dot phrase clearly xxx'ed. Voiding didn't register. Timid equals wrangled revenues from A to B. Sever. Halving. Shelving estimated peculiarities ineffective. Cycled scourings warmed in her hands. Tuningforks quadruple. Inlaid twines aim for synchronized cues from billowing mayflies. She retypes. And retypes. And types.

Faucetless: Codes. Acorns. Disrobed. Ditto. Ditto. A treble clef tattooed on her finger. Debuts recast and crossed off. I peered into an underground stream. I think it would've gone on permanently if void hadn't been misspelled. I could feel her exhaustion. Her disgust. Another day passed. Another neatly spliced tabloid blurb. He said that he couldn't see my reflection in the window. I pointed to where it was. I wasn't interested in reading his thoughts but he seemed to want to read mine. I didn't think he could read them at least I didn't think so at least not the thoughts I didn't want him to read. Another day passed. Purposeful purpose in need of repair. If I trip on the stairs it's well worth the fall. He's not trying to make keys move. They move. He's not trying to tell you what to hear. The hearing is doing the telling. I don't know if I'm moving through the thickness, the thickness that slows everything down.

Rehashing: Doused objects, he embodies a center, a center doubling for vacancy, vacancies only on weekdays. Climbing just above a stopgap crest his position can't be pegged. Naked precipitation. Pieces crumble tiny enough to hide in back pockets. A densely knitted screen separates a bullroarer's infusion from jumbled roses. You can hardly see what the others see, pressed hard, forced to cancel an eternity that should have been thrown away rather than left to dirty the floor. I recognize the burst before the image. The spark before terror condenses. Out of his mouth blows another he.

Trumpeting: Outermost rims summon crestfallen keepsakes. Gutted vigor. Profiles rehouse airtime extensions. Unwelcomed. Unwanted. Ruminating displays cram afterglows. She knows it's circulating through her. A gamble. A tease. Pawned grayscales cite laughable outages. Dated. Written and logged. Moss beds. Blood reefs. Skeleton wagers hunt for rumored shelters. Ascending tempos. Pre-dawn settles into a switchboard reverie.

Blending: A chill. A marbled alcove. A slight rotating glimpse floats and evaporates as they enter before exiting. Thin folds pinned behind glass. A lull settles into an unevenness of crisp grays draped and veiled with inverted orchestration. Breaks in notations never hurried. Inward attentions inexhaustible. I do not argue. Someone is sinking but I don't see them. Left edge. In. Right. Out. I re-walk with brief winding nonchalantly. Lengthiness concise with recorded widths. A hand lifts. A hand falls. Counting segments worthless. A long cloth is tearing inside 1000 boxes. His. Mine. Pile up. Flash, mirror. Topple. Falter. Unceremonious blue streaks cross. I reach the end not finished. I re-walk between second growth and open meadow. Eight dead birds rotting in sand surrounded by sticks to bury deeper. You can't erase turning too soon by walking in front. Lost once. Twice. A blinding glare bellowed before reclining. Outpourings, silhouettes, loop.

Detach: Marked descents crown segueing rotations. Seasonal stakeouts swallow long double looped mechanicalized debris. Trampled arenas intercept blades of hollow swoops. Closings upsurge. Access shrinks. Piles. Mounds. Retract. Fishing lines are not finish lines. Facts don't change foolery. Voided items are tacked onto vacant posts. Sideways. In front of. Clocks rewind.

Drenched: I was rushing somewhere. Shouts from a megaphone could be heard. They were not in agreement. They were not going to relocate. Others just sat. A few argued in silence. He came towards me. I couldn't miss him. He put his face close to mine with a cupped palm and mumbled that his contractor had gone bankrupt. Nobody noticed him slipping out. He'd simply put on his street clothes and walked off carrying some magazines with a novel tucked under his arm. No one followed. No one came after him. Seeing how easy it was he knew he should've done it sooner. He said he only had nightmares when he was up. When he's sleeping he's fine. I was in a pine forest, barefoot. Moonlight. Streetlights. I was pressing a doorbell but then I wasn't. I did what the wind did. But it didn't stop the sounds, not the ones I thought I was hearing but the ones that hadn't yet come. I started whistling. Throat dry. I stood out in the rain with my mouth wide open.

Wedged: Scribbled dissections shoot from blotted depths from smuggled exteriors from trophied imprints. Ovations conjugate the future tense. Seductions materialize. Postured trembles converge. Pause. Dwindle. He's stuck behind his other self. Serene reinventions coil past immersed rubble. Catchwords. Buzzwords. Imitated imitations tagged. Echoes agitate before settling into euphoric gusts.

Turbulence: Shatter deadly thinking. Break deadly ploys. Aside. Set that aside. Locations crescendo when no one listens. 145 or 58. Absolutely too many. Creaking inertia simmers in rotting soil. She showed us how to turn downside inside and outside upside down. Rosewood stalks beat against nonstop delving. It doesn't take long for daylight to reach the unwelcoming curb. He asked about the fermentation of unrest and being wronged. Filtering distances have to be aborted. Another left to cry on the shoulder of an egg. He hunted with her for grasshoppers. She took off her fur hat. It's winter and they're still threshing wheat.

Align: Parachute flares outnumber hijacked sonnets only to be thrown further down. Massive gaps suspended from opaque hooks set everything in motion. Dressed as sandpaper alibis, nonsensical absurdities squirm to win. He and he escort spiky auctioned tipoffs. Timekeepers map shocks and tremors. Inaudible niches switch to the opposite fringe. She wouldn't stay. Not even for a minute. Of course. Of course. Of course.

Quenched: Stand-ins misconstrued for weighty backslides. Vacillating seas transfix sheer trickles into luminescent renderings. Fiery. Somber. Fusible interiorities whirl in overrated giveaways bought for a song. Final counts stored. Encoded. The floor is not a ceiling. To postpone is not to cancel. Partial or practically full. Pseudogalvinzing only fumbles. We got that. Colliding sensations reposition. So many refusals. So many gimmicky newfangled wall-less pages. All is not some. Access whatever unfolds. Whatever collides. Manifestoes won't stay put. They buckle. They break. They sink. Mosaic constellations never cease. Everything is fake except that beeping horn. I second that motion.

Forfeits: Threading tales. Some master it better than others. Some misuse haikus. Some fluff accounts. Some withdrawals are washed and mashed and tumbled dry. Anger can be amusing. Comments brief. Maybe that's better. He drops a white orchid. Disallowing inclusion does make you wonder. I reminded him that his recipe did lack salt. Arms swung. We swam toward a sculpted cellophane cube perched on a sand bar. It was titled "Pointless". But if it's pointless, why is he still insisting on making the point? The winter thaw continues downstream. "Escapades" slipped from my tongue. Voicings emerged without introducing themselves. I listened as close as I could. Fairly broad, slightly irregular, not afar, not near, neither murky nor dim. It made no difference. There was agreement and antagonizing and dispatching. It was hard to decide if it was the a.m. light. I almost descended on a moth's wing.

Tampering: Priceless investment. Safe wisdom. An immensity I can't touch. What defines relevant? What defines longation that even a tightrope walker can't fathom? Diversion. Assault. Accidental stains. One sided reaping should diffuse warnings retrieved. Replicated advice fails to impress her. He's shaking crumbs from his chest. Contented. Acting content. No response. He scowls at me as if I knew whose plan it was. She rattles her tongue. Wiping his burning eyes he points uphill but no one looks. Aghast. He caresses her ever so gently. She doesn't stir. He returns to mopping a violin.

Forestall: Sinking into hollow pools lined with dense thickets she whispered to them and she to us. She said that there was no name for what he had discontinued. He claimed a grassy hill. She an arpeggio. Transferring between here and there went on until morning. She lay on a mat woven from leavings & leftovers. Numbed by token relics dressed in masquerade, the thinking of discarded thoughts spun like a pendulum unable to stop. Little separates unless you desire it. Bypassing only deepens the mess. Dried tears never roll fast enough. Someplace on the agenda they vowed to balance on fingertips, to arrive without traveling. I watched as we entered into the sweep of each colored silk. Flocks of geese flew by as expected. Private. Public. Ramble. Edit. It's already gone.

Slapdash: I sliced rupturing intrusions. I shove inserted rigged stringalongs. I keep unloading crawling sweat. A palette knife steeps in bashes. In pillage. In spoils. She distrusted what rose from plasticized perception. Nonwavering ravages fuse effervescent frost. Outworn preludes prologues preambles launch from backseat barges. Contest winners cook up shriveled linkages retitling them as fruitless blossoms. Droves turn into ruckus. Ruckus into multitudes. Hedgehogs angled from railroad tracks. We can still say it here.

Capacity: Pantomimes filter seasonal shake-ups next to farewell arches crammed into one haptic gulp. Tripling. Multiplying. Sluggish. Jellified. Move closer. There's nothing else. Rushing inward. Pushing out. How little it matters while time is resting. Blazing normalities dowse until parallel lines verticalize. Chin to palms. Palms to chin. Then. It all went blank. Eight cloud changes limit the suspense. The do-s & doing-s. I heard abbreviations tap like a beating heart.

Doggedness: Sounds from the outside were seemingly coherent. Prankster deities slipped jumbled concoctions under doors. Edgings loop. Bait tested. Predictions read faster than decoys. Erasures of memories pull & rise & split like atoms. Neither was sure until eyes met. It was impossible not to agree with disagreeing. Horizons of pallid fields juggle calls against calls. I keep shuffling the deck. Dice twirl like a toy top. I dreamt about thinking of nothing. Beyond. While. Therefore. Returning to the end gains velocity. The momentum of complexity is ready to drop.

Zero: There are not enough incidents of stopping. Knocking door after door is obscene. Restraint starts at the bottom and rises up if not ignored. I guess you could say it's like living two contrasting levels of engagement, never parallel and always switching. Gaps forever prevalent. Wording trimmed too soon can be deleted more easily than redoing circuits of cascading autumn clouds. Pigeons coo. Owls hoot. She saw herself as a doorknob and retreated into her quietude to a location of being imperfect. Interruptions unwanted. Misunderstandings weren't able to halt elongated lines from reaching the landfill. The electricity will return when the throbbing ends. Her hair is already white. Occurrences. Excerpts reduced and others prized. If she goes down the stairs she has to come up. To see what has not yet happened could happen again. The ecstatic moment comes after the fact.

Altering: Not invented, not real, not fact, not too dry. If it can't be recognized it has no label. Detectable measuring nourishes mistakes and laundered ordeals glare like trinkets. The body does roll. It does dunk. It does smother. Explosions revert back to primary maintenance. Unfashionable binds tossed from the nest. Nothing is meant to intertwine. Nothing is meant to end. Nothing is meant to be wiped clear. I bathe in twilights brewing. If we can't remember what we noticed then recollecting lies idle. Swiping up & to the side is not very durable. Better in the dampness I say. It left me not having to pay an odd amount. He pounded the blockade making sure I was looking. I told her she didn't have to write about chewing gum or having sex with the wrong one. I prefer the graininess of not knowing, not the temporary intimacy of sorrow. There was a long line but that's not where it was. You can flood, scramble or forget any part of this.

Creases: Bewilderment impinges upon puzzlement. Lower case lapses into drift driftwood adrift. Seascapes warp from blurry shambles to vintage geometries. The proximity of derailed urgings augments underneath gusty quartets. Welded spheres don't quite convince. Willingly reluctant shoulders touch. Ratios. Quotas. Inedible. Uneatable. Coreless colorless glitches skid. Entire disinfected options slam verses demanding majority. Dis-oriented. Dis-jointed. Aerial lodgings proceed unannounced. He said it was not there and could only be seen by me. I did try to walk on the outskirts and found myself in a stampede, a stampede masquerading as a question.

Crosscuts: Aching for ripeness. Spring's twilight is without a floor plan. That one. Those ones. Barbaric. Lurid. Abbreviated immensities hold & hoard. Thunderous veneer weathers decoys. Turnstile wagers are never symmetrical. It's been told often enough that neutralizing chronicles is an old trick. So common. So very common. Where once was is not where it is. Slender. Angular. Sweltering hues. Siphoned oases double back. Liquidated heaps inhale. Streaks of nothingness are readable from where I sit. Go ahead. Bang more pots. Bang more pans.

www.ingramcontent.com/pod-product-compliance
Lightning Source LLC
LaVergne TN
LVHW041306080426
835510LV00009B/877